Genealogical Writing
in the 21st Century

A Guide to Register Style
and More

Genealogical Writing in the 21st Century

A Guide to Register Style and More

Henry B. Hoff, editor

NEW ENGLAND HISTORIC
GENEALOGICAL SOCIETY

2002

International Standard Book Number: 0-88082-150-7
Library of Congress Control Number: 2002108472

Published by

NEW ENGLAND HISTORIC GENEALOGICAL SOCIETY
101 Newbury Street
Boston, MA 02116-3007
www.NewEnglandAncestors.org

Printed by McNaughton–Gunn, Inc., Saline, Michigan.

Genealogical Writing in the 21st Century

A Guide to Register Style and More

INTRODUCTION

I t is most appropriate that the New England Historic Genealogical Society (NEHGS) publish a guide to genealogical writing — not only because today NEHGS actively publishes books, CD-ROMs, online articles, a journal. and a magazine but because historically so much of American genealogical writing has been shaped and influenced by NEHGS. Since its founding in 1845, NEHGS has played a leading role in establishing genealogical guidelines and determining a genealogical writing style.

The New England Historic Genealogical Society began to set the standard for American genealogical writing in 1847 when the first issue of its quarterly journal, *The New England Historical and Genealogical Register*, was published. The founding members of NEHGS intended not only to preserve important genealogical documents and materials, but also to disseminate such information and make it widely available to NEHGS members. The *Register*, therefore, contained previously unpublished historical and genealogical material, including transcriptions of source material and short genealogies. Looking back, the merits of this undertaking appear obvious, but at the time, the outcome was far from certain. In 1870, Rev. Edmund F. Slafter, author of the Society's "Twenty-Fifth Anniversary Discourse" reflected that "[T]he position to be occupied by this quarterly journal was altogether a new one, like the Society itself it was entering upon an untried experiment. No publication had occupied the same field or undertaken the same work." The longevity of the *Register* is a testament to the success of the endeavor. Published continuously since its first issue, without a single omission, the *Register* is the oldest genealogical journal in the world.

In his 1870 "Discourse" Rev. Slafter also mused on the state of genealogical writing. Prior to the founding of the New England Historic

Genealogical Society in 1845, Rev. Slafter claimed that "scarcely anything had been done in this department. A few rudimentary attempts had been made but they were hardly worthy of the appellation of family histories. Most of them were . . . little more than a collection of names, thrown confusedly together without order or system of arrangement." One of the great contributions of the New England Historic Genealogical Society to the genealogical field was the introduction of an "order and system of arrangement" that provided organization and clarity — in short, the system now known as "*Register* style."

First introduced in the January 1870 issue of the *Register*, the new style was applied to an article on the genealogy of the Sherman family. As editor Albert Harrison Hoyt explained in the "Notes and Queries" section, "[F]or the benefit of future contributors to the *Register*, and perhaps of those about to publish family-genealogies, we have arranged the *Sherman Genealogy*, a portion of which appears in this number of the *Register*, on a plan easily understood, and convenient for reference." In the July 1883 issue of the *Register*, John Ward Dean reported on the use of the "*Register* plan for genealogical records." "It has now been in use thirteen years and has given satisfaction. The Publishing Committee will continue to require genealogies intended for the *Register* to be arranged on this plan." Although modifications have been made to *Register* style over the years to account for changing tastes and changing technologies, it remains fundamentally the same. Today, over 130 years after its introduction, the principles of *Register* style underpin the genealogical writing of the twenty-first century.

Building upon the foundation of *The New England Historical and Genealogical Register* and *Register* style, the New England Historic Genealogical Society has continued to set standards in other areas of genealogical writing. In addition to the *Register*, NEHGS books, CD-ROMs, *New England Ancestors* magazine, and the *NewEnglandAncestors.org* website have all benefited from the application of clear rules of style to sound genealogical scholarship. The accumulated knowledge and experience of the contributors to this volume, all New England Historic Genealogical Society authors and editors, establish anew the importance of following sound guidelines for genealogical writing.

Lynn Betlock
Director of Marketing
NEHGS

PREFACE

This guide is the distillation of opinions from many genealogical authors and editors. *The Chicago Manual of Style* and the NEHGS "house style" rules provided some direction, and the two prior guides published by NEHGS were very helpful. Readers may not agree with everything said in this guide, but all should find the contents to be useful for their genealogical writing, research, and knowledge.

Good genealogical writing in the United States evolved during the twentieth century from the use of implied or little documentation to the requirement of references to reliable sources for every statement of fact that is not public knowledge. Even in the past decade, the style of most genealogical journals changed from imbedded references to footnotes. In the twenty-first century, further changes will occur, no doubt. But good genealogical writing and scholarship will continue to build on the past, making guides like this a helpful contribution to the field.

Grateful thanks for the realization of this guide are due to Gabrielle Stone (Book Publications Supervisor), Carolyn Sheppard Oakley (Editor and Creative Director of *New England Ancestors*), and D. Brenton Simons (Assistant Executive Director) — and to the other authors: Lynn Betlock (Director of Marketing), Helen Schatvet Ullmann, CG (Associate Editor of the *Register*,, Sharon DeBartolo Carmack, CG (genealogical author and editor), Michael J. Leclerc (Director of Electronic Publications), Rod Moody (Electronic Publications Editor), and Christopher Hartman (Director of Book Publications/Newbury Street Press).

Special thanks are due to Elizabeth Shown Mills, CG, CGL, FASG, whose many thoughtful comments and suggestions improved the text greatly. I also wish to thank other genealogical colleagues who reviewed the text and made valuable comments: Joseph C. Anderson II, CG, FASG; Robert Charles Anderson, FASG; Scott Andrew Bartley; David L. Greene, CG, FASG; Eric G. Grundset, MLS; Gale Ion Harris, FASG; Roger D. Joslyn, CG, FASG; David W. Kruger; Helen F. M. Leary, CG, CGL, FASG; Anita A. Lustenberger, CG; Marsha Hoffman Rising, CG, FASG; Gary Boyd Roberts; Clifford L. Stott, AG, CG, FASG; and Helen Schatvet Ullmann, CG.

July 2002   *Henry B. Hoff, CG, FASG*
                                               Editor of The New England Historical
                                               and Genealogical Register

ABOUT NEHGS

New England Historic Genealogical Society

www.NewEnglandAncestors.org
A National Center for Family and Local History
Established 1845

New England Historic Genealogical Society
101 Newbury Street, Boston, Massachusetts 02116-3007
Telephone 617-536-5740
Fax 617-536-7307
Email *nehgs@nehgs.org*

The New England Historic Genealogical Society advances genealogical scholarship and develops the capabilities of both new and experienced researchers of family history by collecting, preserving, interpreting, and communicating — in a variety of accessible formats — reliable genealogical data with emphasis on families and communities connected to New England.

Founded in 1845, the New England Historic Genealogical Society is the oldest genealogical organization in the United States. With over 20,000 members, it is also the largest. NEHGS offers a wide variety of resources for those interested in pursuing their family histories.

The NEHGS Research Library in Boston offers a comprehensive collection of more than 200,000 books, periodicals, and microform materials, as well as an enormous collection of more than one million manuscripts. Its book holdings include nearly all published New England genealogies, local histories, and related periodicals. Its microtext collection, with more than 40,000 items, contains copies of the original town, probate, land, and vital records; city directories; censuses; and immigration records for most of New England and eastern Canada. Beyond New England, family researchers will find many important published and primary sources for other regions, including England, Ireland, Scotland, eastern Canada, French Canada, and continental Europe. NEHGS also provides a highly trained research staff, professional librarians, and volunteers who are eager to help members and patrons in their research.

Many of the resources of the New England Historic Genealogical Society may also be accessed from a distance:

- The NEHGS website, *NewEnglandAncestors.org,* includes helpful research articles, databases with millions of names, and much more.

- Two respected print publications, *The New England Historical and Genealogical Register* and *New England Ancestors*, contribute to genealogical knowledge.

- NEHGS members may borrow books from a 30,000+ volume circulating library by mail.

- An active book and CD-ROM publication program produces approximately twelve new titles a year.

- A range of educational programs, from introductory lectures to extensive research tours, are offered to NEHGS members and patrons in Boston, throughout the country, and abroad.

- NEHGS Research Services offers professional assistance in the form of personal tutorials, photocopying, and research conducted for members and patrons.

For more information about the New England Historic Genealogical Society, please visit *NewEnglandAncestors.org* or call toll-free 1-888-296-3447. NEHGS is located at 101 Newbury Street, Boston, Massachusetts 02116-3007.

Genealogical Writing in the 21st Century

A Guide to Register Style and More

CHAPTER 1

General Advice about Writing and Style

Gabrielle Stone and Carolyn Sheppard Oakley

When writing any kind of work — book, magazine article, journal article — it is important to adhere to a set of guidelines for style. *The Chicago Manual of Style*, published by the University of Chicago Press, is the authoritative work on writing style within the publishing industry. This work not only reviews rules relating to grammar, spelling, and writing style, but it also explains the publishing process from manuscript preparation to printing and binding. At NEHGS, we have standardized our publishing process and style based on the concepts discussed in *The Chicago Manual of Style* and other related publications, such as Elizabeth Shown Mills, ed., *Professional Genealogy: A Manual for Researchers, Writers, Editors, Lecturers, and Librarians* (Baltimore: Genealogical Publishing Co., 2001) and Elizabeth Shown Mills, *Evidence! Citation and Analysis for the Family Historian* (Baltimore: Genealogical Publishing Co., 1997).

NEHGS encourages authors to submit proposals for *The New England Historical and Genealogical Register*, *New England Ancestors* magazine, *NewEnglandAncestors.org*, NEHGS electronic publications, NEHGS book publications, or Newbury Street Press. If the work is accepted, the staff editor of the appropriate department will review with the author the specific guidelines that are elaborated upon in other chapters of this book.

Submitting Manuscripts

In general, text submitted to NEHGS for print publications should be formatted as follows:

1. All manuscripts should be on 8½ x 11 paper, printed on one side only.

2. All manuscripts should be created and saved in the most current version of Microsoft Word. Electronic files may be saved as an

attachment in Word or on a PC-compatible CD-ROM, Zip 100 or 250 disk, or floppy disk. Please contact the specific editor with any other questions regarding the transmittal of the text.

3. The text should be double-spaced (although this is not necessary for the *Register*), and all pages should be numbered sequentially.

4. The font should be Times New Roman, and the text should be in 12 point type.

5. Footnote references in the body of the manuscript should be in superscript.

6. At this point in time, for the *Register* only, create footnotes by using the automatic footnoting feature of your word processing software in 10 point type. For all other NEHGS print publications, footnotes should be in 9 point type and formatted as endnotes.

7. Only one space should be used after periods, question marks, exclamation points, colons, and semicolons. Most computer typefaces, including Times New Roman, are proportionally spaced, and one space is enough to separate sentences visually.

8. All capital letters or underlining to create emphasis should not be used for more than a few words of text.

9. Boldface or italic type and white space between blocks of copy can be used to accentuate breaks in text or create emphasis.

Artwork

When sending images (photographs, maps, illustrations, charts, etc.), please include a *list* of every item sent, a caption or description for each image, an explanation of where the image should be placed within the text, and the *image* itself in hard copy or electronic form. If submitting images in electronic format, discuss the project-specific guidelines with your editor before creating the image files. Please note that the way the image looks in the final product is based mainly on the quality of the original given to NEHGS to reproduce.

Text and Art Permissions

If you quote text from another source in your manuscript, be aware that in certain cases you must obtain permission to use that text. In all cases, direct and indirect quotations of the work of another author *must* be properly cited. Likewise, most images are subject to copyright, and permission to use the image must be obtained from the rights holder, unless you own the original image. This process can take months, so it is best to obtain permission as soon as possible. In addition, it is important to note that there are usually fees involved with obtaining permission for both text and art.

NEHGS editors can in some cases assist with the permissions process. For more information on copyright law, contact the United States Copyright Office, The Library of Congress, 101 Independence Avenue, S.E., Washington, DC 20559-6000; online at *www.loc.gov/copyright*.

General Style Guidelines

It is beyond the scope of this book to enumerate every style issue an author will encounter in preparing a manuscript for submission. This section outlines some of the questions most frequently asked by genealogical authors. Please refer to the three references cited in the first paragraph of this chapter for expanded explanations of these points, as well as answers to more general questions, noting that some of our rules are identical to those rules found in the *Chicago Manual of Style* for example, and some are unique to NEHGS.

When should I use abbreviations?
It is preferable to use abbreviations sparingly, and only in instances in which the author is certain that all readers will be familiar with the abbreviation and its meaning. See Appendix ("Some Abbreviations and Acronyms Used in Genealogy").

Genealogical abbreviations or acronyms are usually formatted without spaces or periods:

> NEHGS, FASG, CG

Do not abbreviate state names in running text. Postal abbreviations should only be used in mailing addresses.

Abbreviate United States only when using it as an adjective. Spell it out whenever it is used as a noun. The two-letter abbreviation (U.S.) for the United States of America uses periods.

How should I style dates?
For the *Register* and compiled genealogies, dates should be written as day, month, year (12 August 2001). For all other NEHGS publications, dates should be written as month, day, year (August 12, 2001). No comma is

needed between a month and a year (August 2001). Commas are required after a year when month, day, and year (or day, month, and year) are used in running text:

> She completed the project on May 25, 2001, and presented her findings to the staff on June 1, 2001.

Do not abbreviate months in running text. Numerical ordinals such as 1st or 2nd should not be used for days; however, they may be used for months in Quaker-style dates (21 7th month 1784).

Decades should be referred to without an apostrophe (the 1820s). Centuries should be referred to in similar style (the 1900s).

When referring to a century, write out the words (nineteenth century); when describing something as belonging to a particular century, use a hyphen (nineteenth-century family Bible or mid-nineteenth-century family history).

What is the best way to write gender-neutral text?
The best way to write copy that applies equally to males and females is to use plurals.

> To be successful, researchers need to attend lectures and practice good organizational skills.

If it is not possible to use plurals, join the pronouns by a conjunction.

> If a student is unable to attend the program, he or she should notify the education department immediately.

In some instances it may be preferable to recast the sentence in the passive voice, even though you should normally avoid using it.

What are the conventions for styling names?
Use a space between two initials. Style three initials or more without spaces between letters.

> J. T. Smith, C.S.D. Jones, and L. Johnson spoke at the meeting.

Jr. or Sr. should be preceded and followed by a comma, but commas are not used with Roman or Arabic numbers — unless personal preference differs.

> Robert S. Brown, Jr.
> Carl B. Taylor III

Carefully double-check the spelling and styling of all names, including personal preferences. Your editor and proofreader may not be familiar with the names in your manuscript and will have difficulty identifying spelling errors.

4

When should I spell out numbers and when should I use numerals?

In general, spell out whole numbers from one through one hundred. Remember to hyphenate where necessary (twenty-one through twenty-nine, etc.). Spell out whole numbers from one through one hundred when they are followed by hundred, thousand, hundred thousand, etc.

Do not observe this rule so strictly that the text becomes inconsistent within a sentence or passage. In reporting ages from a census record, for example, use figures or words consistently throughout.

What frequently used words with alternate spellings should I watch for?

The growth of technology during the past years has brought several new words into the English language, many of which have several different spellings. NEHGS style spells the following words as

> email, online, website, the Web, World Wide Web, and
> Internet

How should I style website and email addresses?

Use standard punctuation when a website address ends a sentence. Most Internet users will be familiar with the basic structure of an address.

Italicize website and email addresses. Do not hyperlink or use enclosures, with the exception of parentheses. Remove any automatic hyperlinking before submitting your manuscript.

Do not add punctuation to an email or Internet address. Do not hyphenate it unless it contains a long word that might naturally break with a hyphen.

Omit "http://" at the beginning of addresses and forward slashes at the end. Most browsers will automatically insert these. This also applies to Web addresses that do not begin with "www."

What are the rules for capitalization?

Capitalization should not be excessive. Generic nouns such as "census" or "tax" or "federal" need not be capitalized, even when used to designate a particular case (e.g., the 1930 U.S. census).

A title is capitalized only when it forms a word group with a following proper noun, even in the same sentence.

> Dick Cheney is vice president of the United States.

> The crowd stood when Vice President Cheney entered the room.

> He served under Admiral Nimitz in Word War II and often heard the admiral talk frankly.

What are the rules for titles of works?

Words in the titles of works in English should all have initial capitals except for articles (unless the first word of the title or subtitle), coordinating conjunctions, and prepositions. It is permissible to correct capitalization of titles. It is also permissible to correct or add punctuation to titles.

Titles of published works (books, periodicals) are italicized. Titles of articles, chapters of books, and unpublished works are enclosed in quotation marks and are not italicized.

> Robert Charles Anderson, George F. Sanborn Jr., and Melinde Lutz Sanborn, *The Great Migration: Immigrants to New England, 1634–1635, Volume I, A–B* (Boston: NEHGS, 1999).

> David Jay Webber, "Major William[2] Bradford's Second Wife: Was She the Widow of Francis[2] Griswold?" *Register* 155 (2001): 245–50.

> John Pynchon, "Hampshire Records of Births: Marriages [&] Deaths," manuscript at the Connecticut Valley Historical Museum, Springfield, Massachusetts.

How should I format quotations?

Long quotations within the text should be set off as block paragraphs with indentation on one or both sides, without quotation marks.

Omissions should be indicated by context-sensitive ellipsis points, separated by spaces. For example, an omission from within a sentence is indicated by three points, which always remain together on a single line of text. Omissions that run over one or more sentence boundaries, on the other hand, will require four points, the first of which follows the last word without a space and indicates a period. In general, ellipsis points are not required at the beginning or end of quotations.

When do I use hyphens, en dashes, and em dashes?

A hyphen (-) joins two words into one.
An en dash (–) expresses a range of numbers or years.
An em dash (—) signifies a major break in thought.

When writing inclusive numbers (such as pages or years), carry over all the digits that change and include at least two digits for the second number (unless in a different century). Such inclusive numbers use an en dash:

> pages 26–29, 147–53, 1,004–05
> years 1887–1915 and 1919–27

An em dash should be set off with a space on either side.

What about other punctuation?

Punctuation is a subject on which volumes have been written. Again, a guide such as *The Chicago Manual of Style* will prove useful in this area. What follows is a summary of some of the particular issues encountered in genealogical writing.

- *Colons*

  A list or a quotation should be introduced by a colon. Capitalize material after a colon if it forms a complete sentence.

- *Commas*

  Within the text, commas should be used sparingly. NEHGS uses the series comma (e.g., French, English, and Italian — rather than French, English and Italian).

  Terms or phrases that are essential for conveying the meaning of the sentence should not be enclosed by commas.

  > The family arrived in 1906 on the ship *Mauretania*.

  But commas are needed when a term or phrase is **not** essential for conveying the meaning of the sentence.

  > Robert Brown, who was the testator's nephew, was named executor in the will.

  The use of "that" and "which" follows comparable rules:

  > The boat that arrived yesterday was on time.

  > The *Mauretania*, which was built in 1900, made its maiden voyage in 1901.

  A clause that begins a sentence should end with a comma.

  > Once Hans made up his mind to emigrate, he could not turn back.

  A single place name does not need commas. But a two-part place name needs two commas.

  > Thomas Ray settled in Ipswich in 1645.

  > Robert Stokes emigrated from Leek, Staffordshire, in 1828.

  A comma can be used to show where the break is in a string of words that otherwise could have more than one meaning.

  > Soon after, the meeting settled down to business.

- *Quotation marks and apostrophes*
  Be careful to use true, "curly" single (') and double ("") quotation marks and apostrophes, rather than the symbols for foot and inch.

  Commas and periods should usually be placed inside double quotation marks. Colons, semicolons, and question marks should be placed outside double quotation marks.

- *Semicolons*
  Use semicolons to separate items in a list that includes commas and to separate closely related clauses in a sentence.

- *Brackets*
  Use brackets to indicate you are adding words or comments to a source or quotation.

CHECKLIST FOR "GENERAL ADVICE ABOUT WRITING AND STYLE"

Before submitting text to NEHGS be sure to

✓ Review and adhere to style, grammar, and spelling guidelines outlined in this text and in the references cited in the first paragraph.

✓ Review the nine points under Submitting Manuscripts.

✓ List any artwork by title, description, source, and placement within text.

✓ Obtain any text and art permissions.

✓ Review the General Style Guidelines.

✓ Review any separate guidelines covered in other chapters of this book.

2

Writing for *The New England Historical and Genealogical Register* and Other Genealogical Journals

Henry B. Hoff and Helen Schatvet Ullmann

W hy do people write articles for *The New England Historical and Genealogical Register* and other genealogical journals? It requires a lot of work, it doesn't pay, and there's the indignity of the editing process during which your carefully constructed article is altered and rearranged. Nevertheless, the *Register* editors receive an average of one new article each week, almost all of which are unsolicited.

Authors have the satisfaction of knowing that their work is preserved and will be of use to researchers in the distant future. Many authors claim that they've sharpened their thinking from the writing process and learned from the editing process. Also, an article can be the best form of query. Experienced authors may publish one or more articles before publishing a full-scale genealogy in order to bring in new information and to publicize the project.

All genealogical journals are looking for new authors. If you see the same authors published again and again in journals, it is probably because they submit articles the editors want, in a form that approximates the journal's style, and they don't need extensive editing.

Content

The *Register* editors are looking for articles on New England subjects or at least with a New England connection. Articles in the *Register* often fall into one of the following four categories:

- Compiled accounts of families
- Problem-solving articles with a brief compiled account
- Immigrant origins with a brief compiled account
- Source material

Nevertheless, the *Register* has published numerous articles that don't fit any of these categories.

In the first three categories, articles usually begin with one or more paragraphs setting out (1) the problem(s), (2) what the author intends to accomplish, and (3) the author's familiarity with previous research on the subject and how the author's contribution fits with what is already known.[1] The author may then present relevant data and analysis, reach conclusions, and finally assemble the results in a brief compiled account (or genealogical summary). A summary of the principal methodology used or type of sources relied upon is desirable, if possible.

> In his *Burnap-Burnett Genealogy*, Henry Wyckoff Belknap confused two men named Thomas Burnap who lived in Reading, Massachusetts, in the late 1600s. . . . Although Belknap correctly quoted a number of early Massachusetts records, he confused the probate records of the two Thomases who died two months apart in 1691. As a result he incorrectly concluded that Thomas, son of John, was the husband of Mary Pearson, and the father of her children. This in turn forced him to conclude that the Mary who was the wife of Thomas, son of Robert, was unidentified. He had, without realizing it, married the cousins to the same woman.
>
> From George H. Perbix, "Thomas Burnap, Husband of Mary Pearson," *Register* 155 (October 2001): 353–56 at 353.

Articles usually begin with one or more paragraphs setting out the problem.

In the fourth category, each type of source material (church records, Bible records, tax lists, account books, etc.) calls for distinctive treatment. In each case, authors should include information on the provenance of the material and perhaps the original transcriber as well as its present location and availability in other formats or media. In most cases the original material should not be rearranged.

The most important aspect of an article is content. The content should be new. If a family's genealogy has not previously been compiled or published, then a full compilation may be warranted. If there is already a good account of the family in print, then an article should just focus on correcting mistakes or presenting new discoveries without repeating much of the reliable material.

While many genealogists write articles on a single line of descent from an immigrant or other early ancestor, the *Register*'s policy is to publish balanced compiled accounts, that is, all descendants of an individual for perhaps two, three, or four generations, or at least all descendants bearing the same

ACCOUNT BOOK AND FAMILY RECORD OF
ROBERT COOK OF NEEDHAM, MASSACHUSETTS

Transcribed by Timothy G. X. Salis

The following records were transcribed from a small (15.5 x 10 cm.), unpaginated, account book recently acquired by the R. Stanton Avery Special Collections Department of NEHGS from a rare book dealer in Pennsylvania. The provenance of this manuscript prior to its acquisition from the dealer is unknown.

The account book originally belonged to Robert Cook (1670–1756) of Needham, Massachusetts. He was born in Boston on 9 December 1670, son of Robert and Sarah (_____) Cook.[1] Robert Cook and Submit Weekes, both of Dorchester, were married on 26 October 1693 at the First Church in Boston.[2] Their first five children were born and baptized in Dorchester.[3] In 1701 or 1702 Robert Cook and his family moved to that part of Dedham that was set off as Needham in 1711.[4] He was active in town government, serving for many years as selectman, treasurer and assessor.[5] Submit (Weekes) Cook died in Needham 18 June 1748, and Robert Cook died there 1 April 1756.[6]

This account book provides more complete information on the children of Robert and Submit (Weekes) Cook than can be gleaned from the vital and church records of Dorchester, Dedham, and Needham, and from the account of the family in Bonniebelle Wright Cook, *The Ancestors of Samuel Cook* (Lima, Okla.: by the author, 1995), 6–7. It also provides an interesting account of what Robert Cook's daughters received at marriage.

---

[1] *Boston Births, Baptisms, Marriages, and Deaths, 1630–1699, [Ninth] Report of the Record Commissioners* (Boston: Rockwell and Churchill, 1883), 114. The account book mentions "sister Elizabeth Smith of Boston" in 1730, but there is no birth record in Boston for an Elizabeth, daughter of Robert Cook. Submit (Weekes) Cook had an older sister, Elizabeth Weekes, born in 1653; however, no marriage is shown for her in Winifred Lovering Holman, *The Ancestry of Colonel Harrington Stevens and His Wife, Frances Helen Miller*, 2 vols. (Concord, N.H.; privately printed, 1948–52), 1:275.

[2] *Boston Births, Baptisms, Marriages, and Deaths* [note 1], 209.

[3] *Dorchester Births, Marriages, and Deaths to the End of 1825, [Twenty-First] Report of the Record Commissioners* (Boston: Rockwell and Churchill, 1890), 38–39, 41, 43–44; William Blake Trask, *Records of the First Church at Dorchester in New England 1636–1734* (Boston: George H. Ellis, 1891), 207–11.

[4] George Kuhn Clarke, *History of Needham, Massachusetts 1711–1911* (Cambridge, Mass.: University Press, 1912), 18, 72. On 1 January 1700/1 the selectmen of Dedham consented to the purchase by Robert Cooke of Dorchester of forty acres of land "granted to William Nahaton neer the vper falls."

[5] *Ibid.*, 648, 658, 675.

[6] Robert Brand Hanson, *Vital Records of Needham, Massachusetts 1711–1845* (Camden, Me.: Picton Press, 1997), 162.

From Register 155 (October 2001): 391–96 at 391. The provenance and present location of source material should be given. Annotations may increase the material's usefulness to readers.

surname. Often some part of such a single-line article solves a particularly interesting problem and can stand alone as an article. The whole work could then be made available to the general public in some other medium, such as *NewEnglandAncestors.org*.

The Process

Submitting Articles to the **Register**

Since the *Register* is published using Microsoft Word, it is best to write your article in a recent version of Word, if possible, and submit it as an email attachment or on a floppy disk with a paper copy. Articles written in other programs and then converted to Word often have serious formatting problems that are extremely time-consuming to resolve.

You do not need to make your manuscript look like the final text. In the footnotes, do not refer to earlier footnotes as their numbers very likely will be changed in the editing process. Give full publication information the first time a source is cited, and from then on use a short title, or author's surname and short title. The editors will provide the necessary cross-references and alterations.

You may want to send the editors photocopies of relevant sources, especially original documents that are important to the article. If the article is source material, you should send photocopies of the originals.

While you might ask the editors whether they would be interested in a certain subject, please do not submit an article until you consider the research complete. The editors probably will ask questions that require further research; however, an article that is essentially finished is far more likely to be accepted and published fairly quickly than one that needs more research.

An article should be submitted to only one journal at a time. If the contents of an article have already appeared in print or will appear in print in some form elsewhere, this should always be communicated to the editors so they are aware. Similarly, if you have previously worked on or published a related article, mention it.

Many authors email the editors in advance to let them know about their article or to ask questions. The current editor is Henry B. Hoff, and his email address is *nehgreditor@aol.com*; however, check the masthead page of the *Register* to verify the most recent contact information. [Helen Schatvet Ullmann is associate editor of the *Register*]. It is always safe to send a paper copy of your article to Editor of the *Register*, NEHGS, 101 Newbury Street, Boston, MA 02116-3007.

Acceptance

The editors' first priority is to produce each issue on time. Due to the high number of articles received, the editors cannot correspond extensively regarding new or potential articles. Most articles need substantial editing, and the editors can deal with only a limited number of articles at a time. Moreover, most articles are sent to one or more consulting editors for evaluation, adding to the time involved.

Once an article is tentatively accepted, the author will receive a permission letter to sign and return. This letter sets out the rights and responsibilities of both NEHGS and the author. Articles that appear in the *Register* are archived on *NewEnglandAncestors.org* and are accessible to members only.

Only a certain number of articles can be accepted. Thus the editors have to choose those they feel are best suited for the *Register*. Sometimes the topic has already been treated in a recent or forthcoming article in the *Register* or another journal. Other times the style of the article is too informal for the *Register* but may be acceptable for another genealogical periodical. Or an

---

VOLUME 155   Whole Number 619   JULY 2001

THE NEW ENGLAND HISTORICAL
AND GENEALOGICAL REGISTER

Contents

Only a certain number of articles can be accepted. The Register *publishes fewer than thirty articles a year.*

article may hinge on an identification that the editors feel is too tentative to publish.

Frequently the editors decide that an article requires major editing, rewriting, and further research to make it ready for publication. They may not want to make a decision about the article until they have time to consider the updated version.

In your cover letter you may want to ask the editors to recommend another journal in case your article is not right for the *Register* or if you want your article to be published sooner than the *Register*'s schedule permits. New England is fortunate in that there are many state and local genealogical journals publishing articles that are of the same high quality as articles in the *Register*. Indeed, the *Register* editors have had many of their own articles published in state and local journals.

Another possible avenue of publication is *NewEnglandAncestors.org*. This is especially appropriate for very long articles and for articles on subjects that may not meet the current needs of the *Register*.

The Editing Process

Once the editors have accepted your article, several months may pass before they are ready to edit it for publication. During this period don't hesitate to email and ask when the editing process may begin. Once the editing process does begin, the editors will have questions that may require you to look at your files or conduct further research. If you will be traveling for any length of time, tell the editors in advance to help prevent delays while you are away.

The editing process usually takes months, with multiple drafts of the articles being emailed back and forth for questions and revisions. Normally, authors will see the final version before publication; however, circumstances sometimes require the editors to make minor changes to an article at the last minute, and there is not time to discuss those changes with the author.

Do not expand your article or change it drastically during the editing process. If you find something important (either positive or negative) during this period, discuss it immediately with the editors. What may appear to be a disaster at first glance may result in a better focused article.

There is nothing embarrassing about making mistakes. All genealogists make them. If you can catch them before they appear in print, so much the better. The *Register* publishes additions and corrections in each October issue.

Style

General Comments

Each statement of fact that is not public knowledge should be cited to one or more reliable sources. This citation may not be to a primary source since a good secondary source with analysis sometimes is more appropriate. When an underlying original source is readily available, it should be consulted instead of relying on a published abstract. This is especially true when the related statement is crucial to your argument. Resources like Torrey's *New England Marriages Prior to 1700* or the *International Genealogical Index* which were intended to be finding aids, should not be cited as sources. Find the original book, article, or document cited, examine it, and then include that original as your source.

> [16] Case of Wm. Graves Jan. 30 – Feb. 4, 1666/7, at pp. 23–30 of transcripts of "Depositions on Cases of Witchcraft Tried in Connecticut, 1662–1693," in the Samuel Wyllys Papers, Brown University Library, Providence, R.I. (and published here with the permission of the Library). A microfilm of photostatic copies of the original depositions is in the Connecticut State Library but it is barely legible. The depositions from this case were published in David D. Hall, *Witch-Hunting in Seventeenth-Century New England: A Documentary History, 1638–1692* (Boston: Northeastern University Press, 1991), 164–69.
>
> From Norbert R. Bankert, "More on the Identity of Abigail (Graves) Dibole, and Her Tragic Death and Suspicions of Witchcraft," *Register* 155 (July 2001): 273–78 at 275.

The original documents examined are cited. Since they have been published, this citation must also be given.

An article should flow logically from one paragraph to the next. Thus a chronological approach may not be best (or even possible) for the entire article. Think carefully about how you are presenting the material. What may be clear to you after working with the family for years may bewilder a reader. A simple chart may clarify complex relationships. When submitting a draft article, you may want to write a few comments to the editors in bold within brackets.

In a cover letter, you may want to inform the editors of relevant sources you reviewed but did not cite (for example, an undocumented website). If your article does not mention a relevant source, especially one contrary to your position, the editors and readers may assume that you had failed to find it.

Avoid "bootstrapping," that is, as the argument is being developed in the article, the author refers to an identification as if it were already proved — when it hasn't been yet.

Besides citing sources, footnotes can convey a lot of other useful information. If a footnote contains more than one source, it may be helpful to indicate which source supports which fact. Footnotes might include an evaluation of a source, a parenthetical remark, or a point that digresses from the flow of the text and yet is important to make. While an article often corrects earlier material in print or manuscript, it may not be necessary to say so in the text. However, the author will want the reader to know that he or she is aware of the conflict, where the outdated or erroneous material has appeared, and perhaps the argument for the correction.

"I" and "we" should be used sparingly in articles. The *Register* editors do not accept a "travelogue" style, that is, a description of the research process, but this style can make for interesting reading and other editors may accept it.

See Chapter 1 of this book, "General Advice about Writing and Style." More detailed advice may be found in works by Patricia Law Hatcher and Elizabeth Shown Mills.[2]

Register Style

The term "*Register* style" refers to the way in which the editors of the *Register* have presented vital and biographical data on families since 1870. The most important points will be presented here and in the illustrations. For variations and nuances, see current issues of the *Register*. Two prior guides published by NEHGS give further details.[3]

While *Register* style may take some getting used to, it provides readers with a standard template for articles, rather than each author's own invented approach. In addition, authors generally find it easier to have a template when writing articles.

The basic unit for presenting in *Register* style is the family group. The earliest head of a family group is assigned the number 1. Following the given name, a superscripted number informs the reader how many generations from the immigrant this person is removed. His or her name is followed by a "lineage line" in italics, giving the name of each progenitor back to the immigrant — and sometimes earlier if the information is known.[4]

For example, an article on Mary Braddock, a fourth generation New Englander, might initially identify her as

MARY[4] BRADDOCK (*Nathaniel*[3], *Robert*[2], *William*[1]), OR

MARY[4] BRADDOCK, daughter of Nathaniel[3] (*Robert*[2], *William*[1]) and Susan (Taylor) Braddock

The account of Mary Braddock that followed would be considered *text* — while the account of her children would be *subtext*. As will be seen in the illustrations, abbreviations, and an abbreviated style are used in subtext.

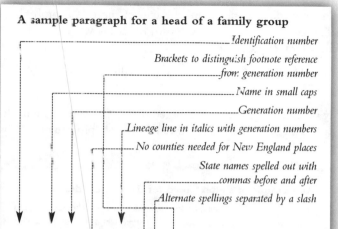

A sample paragraph for a head of a family group

Identification number

Brackets to distinguish footnote reference
from generation number

Name in small caps

Generation number

Lineage line in italics with generation numbers

No counties needed for New England places

State names spelled out with
commas before and after

Alternate spellings separated by a slash

5. **WILLIAM³ MILLS** *(Benjamin², Samuel¹)*, was born at Dedham, Massachusetts, on 2 May 1682,[1] and he died at Needham, Massachusetts, on 9 July 1759.[2] He married first on 28 May 1714, **MARY WARE**, born on 6 April 1691, daughter of Ebenezer and Martha (Herring) Ware.[3] Given the birth of her last child and the date of William's remarriage, she must have died in 1722 or 1723. William was of Needham when he married second, at the Second Church in Roxbury, Massachusetts, on 17 June 1724, **MARY (MOREY) WATSON**,[4] widow of Charles Watson, having married him at Roxbury, Massachusetts, on 2 March 1714/5.[5] She was born at Roxbury on 11 August 1682, daughter of Thomas and Susanna (Newell) Mowry/Morey.[6] She was the "Widow of William Mills Senr" who died at Needham on 3 October 1759.[7]

Note that places generally precede dates of events and that abbreviations are not used. Note also that each piece of information has a corresponding footnote. A date before 1752 and between 1 January and 24 March should be expressed as a double-date (e.g., 2 March 1714/5), or as 2 March 1714[/5] if inferred from the context, or as 2 March 1714[/5?] if uncertain.

After Mary Braddock's name and lineage line or parentage would come her place of birth and date of birth, assuming they are known. If there is a question about place of birth, it may be preferable to put the date of birth first. So, for example:

Born at Marlborough, Massachusetts, about 1718

BUT

Born about 1718, probably at Marlborough, Massachusetts

Her place and date of death and burial may come next or may be toward the end of the text, depending on circumstances. For example, if Mary Braddock outlived three husbands and evidence of her date and place of death requires discussion, toward the end of the text is probably a better place. Frequently an exact date of death is not known and a statement like the following is appropriate:

> Died between 2 July 1772 (date of will) and 3 September 1772 (probate of will)

Usually statements should be footnoted the first time they are made; however, there will be instances like "date of will" or "probate of will" when it

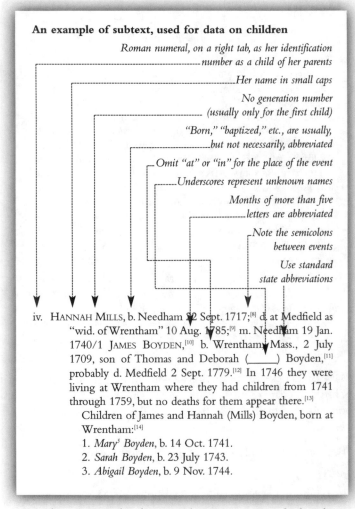

An example of subtext, used for data on children

Roman numeral, on a right tab, as her identification number as a child of her parents

Her name in small caps

No generation number (usually only for the first child)

"Born," "baptized," etc., are usually, but not necessarily, abbreviated

Omit "at" or "in" for the place of the event

Underscores represent unknown names

Months of more than five letters are abbreviated

Note the semicolons between events

Use standard state abbreviations

iv.   HANNAH MILLS, b. Needham 22 Sept. 1717;[8] d. at Medfield as "wid. of Wrentham" 10 Aug. 1785;[9] m. Needham 19 Jan. 1740/1 JAMES BOYDEN,[10] b. Wrentham, Mass., 2 July 1709, son of Thomas and Deborah (_____) Boyden,[11] probably d. Medfield 2 Sept. 1779.[12] In 1746 they were living at Wrentham where they had children from 1741 through 1759, but no deaths for them appear there.[13]

Children of James and Hannah (Mills) Boyden, born at Wrentham:[14]

1. *Mary⁵ Boyden*, b. 14 Oct. 1741.
2. *Sarah Boyden*, b. 23 July 1743.
3. *Abigail Boyden*, b. 9 Nov. 1744.

Note that commas rather than semicolons separate events (birth and death) for the spouse. Including the surname for each child makes an electronic search feasible. If biographical information on a child is extensive, it may be better to also make him or her the head of a separate family group.

is evident the citation will be given later in the text.

Place and date of marriage should follow, with an indication of first or later marriage. For example:

> Married first at the Bozrah Congregational Church, Norwich, Connecticut, on 28 April 1740, WILLIAM EDGERTON.

Only partial information may be available, and again you want to indicate why you are making each statement. For example:

> Married before 12 February 1742 (when their first child was baptized), perhaps at Norwich, Connecticut, where her parents were living.

The identification of the spouse follows his or her name, and it is usually in the same order as above. Continuing this example, the spouse might be

> WILLIAM EDGERTON, born at Norwich on 20 April 1715, died before 2 January 1765 (when his wife remarried), son of Richard and Lucy (Smith) Edgerton.

Parents of spouses should be mentioned, as it makes the article more complete and useful to more readers.

After these one or two paragraphs, biographical information on the couple follows, usually in chronological order. Finally their children are listed in subtext. Illustrations show the conventional order of data, punctuation, and abbreviations typical of *Register* style. Each child has a lower-case Roman numeral, and any child carried forward is given an Arabic numeral, following from the number assigned to the last child carried forward in the previous family group.[5] Grandchildren may be listed here, depending on the scope of the article.

Be consistent in your overall style, even if not conforming to *Register* style in all respects. For example, citations should include place of publication; if you want to add the publisher, do so for all citations. Some authors make their own checklists for overall style and completeness.

Authors should be aware that genealogy computer programs claiming to generate a "*Register*-style report" are usually quite deficient. Such a report, if used, will need substantial editing by the author prior to submission in Word.

Other Journals

Other American genealogical journals have comparable styles. It is best to write an article with a specific journal in mind. Even if you end up giving your article to a different journal the editor should be able to convert it to the style of that journal, as long as you have been consistent.

CHECKLIST OF "WRITING FOR *THE NEW ENGLAND HISTORICAL AND GENEALOGICAL REGISTER* AND OTHER GENEALOGICAL JOURNALS"

☑ Does the content of your article fit with *Register* preferences?

☑ Is the content of your article new?

☑ Are you using Microsoft Word?

☑ Is your research complete?

☑ Are your footnotes complete?

☑ Is each statement of fact that is not public knowledge cited to one or more reliable sources?

☑ Does your article flow logically from one paragraph to the next?

☑ Does your article include material that should be moved from text to footnotes — or omitted entirely?

☑ Does your article conform to *Register* style?

☑ Have you been consistent in your overall style?

Notes

1 Margaret F. Costello and Jane Fletcher Fiske, *Guidelines for Genealogical Writing: Style Guide for* The New England Historical and Genealogical Register *with Suggestions for Genealogical Books* (Boston: NEHGS, 1990), 1–2.

2 Patricia Law Hatcher, *Producing a Quality Family History* (Salt Lake City: Ancestry, 1996); Elizabeth Shown Mills, *Evidence! Citation & Analysis for the Family Historian* (Baltimore: Genealogical Publishing Co., 1997); Elizabeth Shown Mills, ed., *Professional Genealogy: A Manual for Researchers, Writers, Editors, Lecturers, and Librarians* (Baltimore: Genealogical Publishing Co., 2001).

3 Costello and Fiske, *Guidelines for Genealogical Writing* [see note 1]; Thomas Kozachek, *Guidelines for Authors of Compiled Genealogies* (Boston: Newbury Street Press, 1998).

4 Superscript style for pre-American ancestry differs; see current issues of the *Register* for examples.

5 The "Modified *Register*" style (or system) assigns an Arabic numeral to all children in a family, and indicates those carried forward by a plus sign. This is the system currently used by *National Genealogical Society Quarterly,* and is now called the NGSQ style (or system). For further information and discussion about nuances of use, see Joan Ferris Curran, Madilyn Coen Crane, and John H. Wray, *Numbering Your Genealogy: Basic Systems, Complex Families, and International Kin*, National Genealogical Society Special Publication No. 64 (Arlington, Va.: NGS, 1999).

CHAPTER 3

Writing for *New England Ancestors* and Other Popular Genealogical Magazines

Sharon DeBartolo Carmack

There's no better time to be a genealogical writer. With many magazines that publish articles for a popular audience and one geared for professional genealogists, you can pick and choose where you'd like to see your byline. Maybe you'll want to see your work appear in all of them. While all of these publications have the goal of reaching the beginning genealogist as well as the established researcher, few people subscribe to or read all of them. That means each publication reaches a slightly different audience. But all of these magazines need good writers who know how to meet deadlines, and several of them will pay you for your submission. So how do you break into the popular genealogical writing market? It's really not that difficult to go from article idea to bylined author.

Your Article Ideas

I'll never forget the first time I chatted with Elizabeth Shown Mills, CG, FASG, editor of the *National Genealogical Society Quarterly*, when I became editor of the *Association of Professional Genealogists Quarterly*. We were talking about article ideas. She said, "Coming up with ideas is easy. It's finding good, qualified writers to write them." Elizabeth didn't know it at the time, but I was inwardly shaking, thinking I would surely run out of ideas by the second or third issue. That was in 1989, and she was right: in more than thirteen years as a writer and editor, I've had to come up with ideas not only for articles I wanted to write but also ideas for articles to suggest to writers. So far, the well hasn't gone dry.

One of the best ways to get ideas for articles is to read or scan all the popular magazines and attend national conferences. You'll notice that there are only a few core topics in genealogy and most of them revolve around types of sources, methods for using sources, and research/problem-solving techniques. So what could be left for you to write about? Hasn't everything been covered already? To a degree, yes, but each person can bring a new spin to a core topic. Many people have written on or lectured about the census, for example, but each approaches it a bit differently. One might deal with the basics of census research, another might cover the use of pre-1850 censuses, another focuses on correlating census data through the decades, and yet another will address using censuses online. Your job is to find an approach that someone hasn't used yet, or that you use differently.

After you establish yourself with a magazine and an editor, don't hesitate to ask that editor for ideas he or she would like to see covered. In fact, editors often have ideas for articles and then look for people to write them. Let your editor know of your willingness to research and write on a variety of topics and ask to be kept in mind for assignments.

Finding the Right Market for Your Article

Once you have an idea for an article, the next step will be to decide which magazine your article is best suited for. Almost all the popular genealogical magazines offer writer's guidelines. Request them and study the types of articles in each of the magazines. Who are the magazine's readers? *New England Ancestors*, for example, goes to all members of the New England Historic Genealogical Society and therefore reaches people who are serious about genealogy, from beginner to advanced. On the other hand, the majority of *Family Tree Magazine* readers are beginners in genealogy, so articles are written with that audience in mind. Those who subscribe to the Federation of Genealogical Societies' (FGS) *Forum* presumably have an intermediate to advanced research skill level.

Along with the level of genealogist each magazine reaches, also note the types of articles. *Family Tree Magazine* does not publish case studies; it focuses on how-to articles. The FGS *Forum* gears many of its articles and columns to the needs of genealogical society members and officers. Readers of the *Association of Professional Genealogists Quarterly* are not only genealogists who take clients, but librarians, instructors, heir tracers, and genealogical book vendors. *Heritage Quest* publishes how-tos, "light" case studies, and human-interest stories, as do *Ancestry, Family Chronicle*, and *Everton's Family History*. *Genealogical Computing* caters to "techno-genealogists." *New England Ancestors* prefers articles that focus on the New England region, but also publishes general articles covering all parts of the country.

Popular genealogical magazine editors want articles written in a conversational tone, as I've written this chapter. That is, address your reader as "you," find a good "hook" for the opening paragraph that will draw in the reader, add some appropriate humor, use contractions, end sentences with prepositions as you would in conversation, and avoid the passive voice.

Be careful of how much you insert yourself into the article. While there is nothing wrong with telling the reader how you did something, readers are more interested in how *they* can do something. This chapter is a perfect example. I could have written it on how I've been published in popular genealogical magazines, since it's based on my experiences as a popular writer and editor, but who really cares? You want to know how *you* can get published in popular genealogical magazines. So the chapter is you-focused, not I-focused.

Going Rates for Magazine Articles

If you are supplementing your genealogical income as a writer, then part of your decision as to where to send an article may be based on what the magazine pays. You can earn from zero to $800 for an article. Only one magazine pays upon acceptance of the article; all of the others pay upon publication, which means you may not see a paycheck for several months if the article isn't published right away.

But don't let pay cloud your vision if your goal is to write, get published, and make a name for yourself in genealogy. The field of genealogy, while rapidly becoming commercialized, still relies heavily on its volunteer force. If you can't volunteer in the organizations you belong to because you are homebound or have a full-time job, then consider writing for the society's publication as your contribution. Sometimes just the prestige of being published in a highly respected magazine, such as *New England Ancestors*, is as valuable as receiving monetary remuneration, plus you'll be adding to your bibliography.

Querying the Editor

Most genealogical editors prefer that you send them a "query" rather than a completed manuscript of an article. This means you pitch your article idea in a letter or email, asking if the editor would be interested in having you write the article. There is no need to spend your time and energy writing an article that no magazine is interested in. It's a much softer blow to your writer's ego to have an idea rejected than a completed article.

Keep your query short and to the point. A good query is no longer than a single hard-copy page. Your letter should

- address the editor by name. "To Whom It May Concern" is also acceptable, but do not use "Dear Sir."
- grab the editor's attention in the opening paragraph as you would in the first paragraph of an article.
- clearly state your article idea, i.e., what the article is about, what your slant is, why this is a hot topic, how many words you envision the article will be, and suggestions for possible illustrations.

- state why you are the best person to write this article (give your qualifications).
- tell when you can deliver the article.

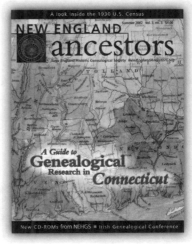

Always double-check your query letter or email for errors and typos, and if using regular mail, include a self-addressed, stamped envelope. Some editors will respond within a week; others may take several months to respond.

Can you send simultaneous queries to editors? In other words, can you send the same query or completed manuscript to more than one editor at the same time? While some editors don't mind this and ask only that you make them aware that this is a simultaneous submission in your cover letter, others frown upon the practice.

Assuming the editor likes your article idea, he or she may offer you a boiler-plate contract or publishing agreement for you to sign. There are many good books that explain publishing contracts, such as Brad Bunnin and Peter Beren's *The Writer's Legal Companion,* 3rd edition (Perseus Books, 1999). A good rule, however, is not to sign anything you don't understand.

Researching and Writing the Article

Mystery writer Sandra Brown said, "The worst piece of advice I was ever given was to write about what I know. I took stock of what I knew and, from a creative standpoint, none of it was very stimulating. . . . I have no personal knowledge of, or experience with, paramilitary hate groups, or heart transplantation, or escapees from maximum security prisons, or what it's like to be profoundly deaf. But I've written about all these topics, and the books became best sellers." While we may not be writing mystery best sellers like Sandra Brown, we can apply her quote to genealogical writing, too. Genealogists by their nature are researchers. If you are assigned a topic or just have an interest in a topic, research it well enough to write a popular article about it. Your research should include interviewing colleagues who know more than you do about the topic so you can quote them as experts in your article.

The more you write, the quicker you will become at researching and writing articles. And the more you write, the better you will become at judging how long it will take you to research and write an article. You will find it helpful to outline your article, either on paper or mentally, before you begin writing and to help guide your research.

As you study the genealogical magazines, you'll notice some of the same writers' names cropping up. How do they write so many articles? They have learned to write fast David Fryxell's *How to Write Fast (While Writing Well): A Guide to Speed, Organization, Concentration, Problem-Solving, and Creativity* (Cincinnati: Writer's Digest Books, 1992) is an excellent resource if you want to do a lot of writing for popular genealogical magazines. This book will help you juggle multiple writing projects and show you how to get the most information out of the research you need in order to write on a topic for a popular genealogical magazine.

As you are writing the article, stay conscious of the word count. The word limit the editor gives you in your contract is there for a reason. The editor knows exactly how much space 3,000 words take up in the magazine. Significantly going over or under the limit won't endear you to an editor.

Keep your audience in mind, too, as you write. Articles for popular genealogical magazines are meant to inform and instruct. Don't forget to include basic information for the reader, such as mentioning a website *and* its URL, giving an acronym *and* spelling it out at the first mention, referencing a book *and* including the publisher information.

The Dreaded "D" Word

All magazines run on deadlines, and the editor will give you one when he or she sends you a contract. When you are discussing the article with the editor or negotiating the contract, if the deadline is unrealistic, don't be afraid to ask for a later date. Deadlines tend to creep up faster than you expect. Better to say something early on and ask for more time, than miss the date.

To avoid missing your deadline, put the date in red on your calendar — but mark it for at least a week earlier than the deadline the editor gave you. That way you'll be early with your article, and your editor will love you. If the deadline is for the first of a month, always mark a due date in the previous month. You don't want to be caught by surprise when you flip your calendar page to a new month and discover you've got an article due on the first, and you haven't even begun thinking about it yet.

Missing a deadline has a snowball effect on everyone who works on the magazine. Sure, everyone misses a deadline now and then, but if it's more than a day or two late, or you are habitually late — even if you keep the editor apprised — your editor will probably start favoring other writers who make deadlines sacred dates. Those writers whose names you see regularly in popular genealogical magazines? They're always getting articles published because they always meet their deadlines.

Submitting Your Article

The writer's guidelines for the magazine you're writing for should tell you the house style, how to format your manuscript, and how to submit it to the editor (on a computer disk with a paper copy or by email attachment). "House style" is how the magazine makes each article look consistent within the publication. For example, some magazines may spell out numbers one through ninety-nine, while others will only spell out numbers one through ten, then use numerals. Or, one magazine might use the series commas (that is, a comma separating all elements in a series, such as red, white, and blue), while another may not use the series comma (red, white and blue). Some may use endnotes; others prefer references be within the text or as part of sidebars.

One pet peeve of many editors is the writer who formats the manuscript to match the publication's look. Most editors want old fashioned-looking manuscripts even if you are submitting it electronically, that is, double-spaced, no columns, printed on one side of 8½ x 11 paper, with one-inch margins all around. Don't use fancy fonts: Times New Roman, 12 point is fine, and don't add graphics to the manuscript. Send these in a separate file or print them out on a separate page.

After you submit your article, it will go through copyediting. This is where the editor or a copyeditor reads your article for flow and continuity, tightens sentences, fixes any grammatical problems, adjusts the article to house style, or possibly reorganizes the article. Maybe the third paragraph would work better as the first paragraph, or a section toward the end of the article flows better in the middle. Depending on your writing skill, how closely you've matched the style and voice of the magazine, and how light or heavy-handed the editor is with the red pen, your article may look almost identical to the way you submitted it, or it could look as if it was rewritten. Don't be too alarmed. All articles get edited, even those written by experienced, professional writers. Writers are usually too close to their material to see how an article can be improved. Of utmost importance, however, is that the editor hasn't inadvertently changed the meaning of any of your sentences or your article. Unfortunately, not all magazines return the copyedited manuscript to the writer. This is something you need to ask about when you negotiate your contract. If you do get to see the copyedited manuscript, inform the editor if your meaning has been changed during copyediting.

After copyediting, the article is laid out as it will appear in the magazine. If you are given the opportunity to review at this stage, the pages are called either "galleys" or "page proofs." If your contract does not stipulate an author review at the page proof stage, ask the editor if you can review them. While the magazine will have proofreaders to check for typos and layout problems, it always makes an author feel more comfortable to see the article right before it goes to press. When the editor mails, faxes, or emails you the pages, review and return them with any corrections by the date the editor tells you. Keep in mind that at the page proof stage, you cannot make any major changes or additions. You may only correct typos or glaring errors. Adding even one sentence might affect the pagination and subsequently everything that follows your article.

Basking in the Byline

Not long after you've reviewed the page proofs, you'll receive the actual magazine with your article published. Nothing can compare to that feeling of seeing your name in print for the first time or the hundredth time. You'll carry around the issue everywhere you go and proudly show it to friends and family. But don't bask too long. You've got more articles to write!

CHECKLIST FOR "WRITING FOR *NEW ENGLAND ANCESTORS* AND OTHER POPULAR GENEALOGICAL MAGAZINES"

- ☑ Survey and study the popular genealogical magazines.

- ☑ Pick topics that interest you, and then see how you can put a new spin on them.

- ☑ Review the popular magazines and decide which ones you want to pitch your article idea to based on your topic, circulation, pay, and prestige.

- ☑ Query the editor in one page, presenting your article idea, your qualifications, and your proposed delivery date.

- ☑ Once the article idea has been accepted, begin researching and writing the article.

- ☑ Remember, the more you write, the better and quicker at it you'll become.

- ☑ Be a writer editors love: Stick to the word limit and submit your article by the deadline, early if possible.

- ☑ Submit the manuscript according to the magazine's writer's guidelines.

- ☑ Ask to review copyedits or page proofs, then do so in a timely manner.

- ☑ Proudly show off your published article, then begin the process all over again!

MORE INFORMATION ON *NEW ENGLAND ANCESTORS*

NEW ENGLAND HISTORIC GENEALOGICAL SOCIETY
101 Newbury Street
Boston, MA 02116-3007
email: *magazine@nehgs.org*
website: *www.NewEnglandAncestors.org*

New England Ancestors magazine offers a vibrant and exciting new approach to genealogy in New England and throughout the United States. Appropriate for family historians of every level, this popular 64-page bimonthly magazine is a benefit of NEHGS membership.

Frequency: bimonthly. *Circulation:* approximately 20,000. *Rights:* Requires a signed agreement granting NEHGS the right to archive the text of the article in a members-only area of *www.NewEnglandAncestors.org*; permission to reprint and/or republish the article, as originally published in *New England Ancestors*, at any time and in any manner in keeping with the mission of NEHGS, including compilations and electronic format; and the author's agreement not to publish the article in any other journal or magazine, or by any electronic means, without first consulting the editors of *New England Ancestors* and citing *New England Ancestors*. *Average length of articles:* 1,200–2,750 words. *Submissions:* Query or submit completed manuscript. Query by email. Response time to query: 1–2 months. Does not accept simultaneous submissions and rarely previously published submissions. Submit article electronically on disk and hard copy. Writer's guidelines available by mail or email.

CHAPTER 4

Writing for *NewEnglandAncestors.org* and Other Websites

Michael J. Leclerc and Rod Moody

T he first consideration when writing for any publication is to think about how the reader will approach and interpret the text. Style guidelines for grammar, punctuation, capitalization, names, dates, quotes, statistical presentations, etc., remain essentially the same for all NEHGS publications. Please refer to the chapters that illustrate style guidelines for print publications for that information. This chapter will cover the differences between writing for the Internet and writing for print publications.

Writing for an online audience is similar to writing for a periodical. Most readers will scan until they find something that catches their eye. The majority of online readers are searching for information that is easy to locate, easy to digest, and easy to print. With this in mind, try to present the text in a way that will fulfill these criteria.

Article Length

The amount of text that is displayed on a single page of a website is important. Although cable and DSL modems are gaining in popularity, a significant number of Internet users continue to use modems that operate at slower speeds. If a lengthy article is displayed on a single web page, it could take a considerable amount of time to download that page. This delay defeats the main purposes of web content — ease of use and quick results. It is up to the editor to decide how to split up lengthy articles into separate pages. Writers need to realize that long articles will be divided, and they should plan their content accordingly. If there is no clear line of division, the editor may ask the author to rewrite the article. Authors tempted to "write long" should also keep in mind that the vast majority of Internet users will not read an article word for word. As previously noted, most readers of Web content prefer to scan the page. The **maximum** length for any article posted on a single page of *NewEnglandAncestors.org* is three thousand words.

Enhancements

When designing and formatting a web page, you can employ several techniques to attract the reader's attention. The most common are listed below.

Hyperlinks
Hyperlinks enable readers to go instantly to an area that interests them most with a click of a mouse. A hyperlink is created in HTML, which renders the normal text into underlined "clickable" text. Hyperlinks can be used to reference a different location on the Internet or to let the reader "jump" to a different location on the same web page. Hyperlinks to email addresses are also commonly used. Here is an example from Maureen Taylor's article "Scoundrels in Rhode Island" (*NewEnglandAncestors.org*, November 9, 2001) that shows how hyperlinks can help the reader and the author:

> Civil and criminal court cases kept by the Rhode Island Supreme Court Judicial Records Center can be a gold mine for researchers. Their archives contain civil and criminal court cases (1671–1900), divorce cases (1749–1900), and some naturalization papers (1793–1974). Online order forms are available on their website for specific requests, but for general information about the archives' holdings, send an email request to them. All court cases after 1900 must be requested via regular mail. See their website for further details.

In the above example, clicking on the first underlined text takes readers to the Judicial Records Center website where they can download an online order form. Readers may also click on the underlined "email request" text, which will automatically launch the email program with the address already filled in. Notice also that the last sentence advises readers to see the website for further details, as there are far too many details to be included in the article.

Another valuable use for hyperlinks is to jump to other pages within the same site. When writing for *NewEnglandAncestors.org*, think in terms of what hyperlinks you can provide that would be beneficial to the reader. For instance, in Patricia Law Hatcher's article on land records, "Land Records: New England's Under-Appreciated Resource" (*NewEnglandAncestors.org*, February 15, 2002), she urged readers to visit other areas of the NEHGS website for additional information by adding hyperlinks, as shown in the following example:

> Land records are also voluminous. The indexes alone might require many rolls of microfilm. On a recent NEHGS trip to the Family History Library in Salt Lake City, NEHGS Librarian David Dearborn and I agreed that, for this reason, focusing on land records is a highly

efficient use of a researcher's time in Salt Lake City.
Tip: *Learn more about NEHGS Tours and Education events.*

In Connecticut, Rhode Island, and Vermont, deeds are maintained at the town level. In Maine, Massachusetts, and New Hampshire, they are at the county level, although original grants are at the town level.

Tip: *To learn more about the location of New England land records, see Marcia D. Melnyk's* Genealogist's Handbook for New England Research.

In her first paragraph, Patricia Law Hatcher indicates that researching land records in Salt Lake City is a worthwhile endeavor. She then provides a link to the page where interested readers could sign up for a NEHGS research tour to Salt Lake City. Next, she writes about where the records are kept in various New England states and follows by adding a link to the NEHGS online book store, where the reader can buy books that explain New England research in greater detail.

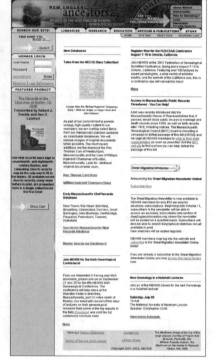

Tables and Bulleted Lists
Bulleted lists are an excellent way to attract a reader's attention while presenting the information in an easy-to-read format. Just imagine how the example below would look without the bullet points!

Court Records
The court records found at the Archives are an excellent source of information about the lives of the people of the state. Like the petitions, these are original records.

- Provincial Period (pg. 52) 1630s through 1772
- Hillsborough County (pg. 9) 1772 through the first decade of the 1900s, depending on the series
- Merrimack County (pg. 12) from its inception in 1823 through 1900
- Rockingham County (pg. 10) 1772 through 1920
- Strafford County (pg. 32) 1780 through 1899, which are not yet processed
- Sullivan County (pg. 35) from incorporation in 1827 through 1919
- Belknap County (pg. 10) 1840 through 1899
- Grafton County (pg. 9) 1773 to 1899, partially indexed

Tables can divide complex information that is not easily readable as a paragraph into a format that makes sense to everyone. Here is an example in which an author included a series of important dates for the reader to note:

> Sleepytown was settled in 1763, organized April 26, 1770, but not incorporated as a town until June 23, 1784. On June 24, 1826, it was divided to form West Sleepytown, East Sleepytown, and Sleepyville Junction. The name of West Sleepytown was changed to Sleepytown on March 12, 1830, and part of Dullsville was annexed on February 22, 1838. On February 10, 1845, there was a set off to form Boringsboro, and on June 30, 1846, another set off was made to form Snoozefield.

For the final copy, this information was transferred into a table and introduced by a subheading:

Chart 1: Important Dates for Sleepytown Researchers

1763	Settlement of Sleepytown
April 26, 1770	Sleepytown organized
June 23, 1784	Incorporated as a town
June 24, 1826	Sleepytown divided to form West Sleepytown, East Sleepytown, and Sleepyville Junction
March 12, 1830	Name of West Sleepytown changed to Sleepytown
February 22, 1838	Part of Dullsville annexed to Sleepytown
February 10, 1845	Set off made to form Boringsboro
June 30, 1846	Set off made to form Snoozefield

Subheadings

Subheadings are essential to any online article divided into particular sections. Another example, from Barbara Mathews' column "Manuscript Family Records in Connecticut" (*NewEnglandAncestors.org*, February 1, 2002), shows just how effective they can be:

**Ancestry Service Pedigrees
at the Connecticut Society of Genealogists**
The Ancestry Service is a collection of the pedigree charts of members of the Connecticut Society of Genealogists. These are kept in three-ring binders at the Society's library in East Hartford and bound into a continuous set of volumes ordered by the membership number of the submitter. Three indexes cover the pedigrees, each focusing on a particular run of membership numbers. Each name in a pedigree chart is indexed to a membership number and the page within that member's pedigree chart. The index to the first series has been published. Currently, the Society's journal, *The Connecticut Nutmegger*, is

publishing sections of the index to the first series in each issue.

The library of the Connecticut Society of Genealogists is open Monday through Friday, 9:30 a.m. to 4 p.m. It is open both to members and non-members alike.

Connecticut Society of Genealogists Library
175 Maple Street
East Hartford, Connecticut 06033
860-569-0002

Family Files at the Ferguson Library
The Ferguson Library in Stamford, Connecticut, is the "home" library of the Connecticut Ancestry Society. There are six file cabinet drawers of family files as well as a local history collection. The Connecticut Ancestry Society also houses a pedigree collection at the Ferguson, the contents of which were contributed by their members.

The Ferguson Library
One Library Place
Stamford, Connecticut 06904
203-964-1000

The Julia Brush Collection at the Cyrenius Booth Library
The public library in Newtown, Connecticut, is the repository of the Julia Emeline Clark Brush collection of genealogical materials. Items of interest include transcripts of probate, land, vital, cemetery, and town records for many surrounding towns in western Connecticut and eastern New York. There are also family files and local history scrapbooks. This collection is housed in the basement of the library.

Cyrenius Booth Library
25 Main Street
Newtown, Connecticut 06470
203-426-2533

Note the clear division between each collection shown and the easy-to-locate contact information.

Images
Authors are encouraged to submit or suggest images with their articles, when appropriate. Images should be free of copyright restrictions or the author should

Six of - The Scholars

obtain a written letter of consent from the copyright holder and forward it to the website editor. Images should be sent in "tif" format via email or on disk to the editor. All images should be scanned at 300 dpi.

Endnotes

All source citations should be listed at the end of the document as endnotes. Do not insert between paragraphs or at the end of individual pages.

Submission Requirements

All articles should be submitted as Microsoft Word document attachments.

Formatting

Publishing online requires different formatting than traditional publishing techniques. It is important to keep these things in mind when you are writing for the Internet.

Fonts

Serif fonts, such as Times New Roman, are the standard for print publishing. For electronic publishing, however, sans-serif fonts should be used. Sans-serif fonts are much more readable on a computer screen because the lines of the letters are cleaner without the serifs. Arial font is preferred and type should be 12 point for body copy (never more than 14 point, and never less than 10 point).

Underlining

Items on a web page that are underlined are hyperlinks to bring you to another page. Text should never be underlined unless it is meant to be a hyperlink. Doing so can cause extensive confusion for the reader.

Italics

Italicized fonts appear differently onscreen than they do in print. Limited italics can be used to bring emphasis; but, extended italics should not be used in electronic publications. Standard rules should be followed, however, such as italicizing the names of published works, when the situation warrants.

All Caps/Small Caps

Using all caps online make the text stand out dramatically. IT IS THE EQUIVALENT OF SHOUTING! It is very harsh and difficult to read. Extended text should never be set as all caps or small caps.

CHECKLIST FOR "WRITING FOR *NEWENGLANDANCESTORS.ORG* AND OTHER WEBSITES"

- ☑ Is the article the appropriate length?

- ☑ Does the article include subheadings for easy division?

- ☑ Are there hyperlinks to other resources?

- ☑ Is information presented as a table or bulleted list where appropriate?

- ☑ Are there images to accompany the article?

- ☑ Are all images copyright-free, or do you have a signed permission letter from the copyright holder?

- ☑ Are all images scanned at 300 dpi?

- ☑ Are sources documented and cited as endnotes, not footnotes?

CHAPTER 5

Writing Genealogical Books

D. Brenton Simons, Gabrielle Stone,
and Christopher Hartman

hy write your family genealogy or other genealogical book? For years you have been assembling notes, files, binders, boxes, and even filing cabinets on your family or other genealogical topic. So the next natural step is to produce a manuscript that presents your work in a concise, readable, and consistent format.

Thoughts for Authors and Potential Authors

Let your thoughts focus and develop while you are researching. What seems fascinating now may seem less so after gaining more perspective on your research.

Most of the information in your proposed book should be new. If a branch of your family history already is in print, explore areas that have not yet been researched. This helps expand the existing body of knowledge and avoids unnecessary overlap.

Consider the usefulness and potential audience of the book. A book on your ancestry would be of interest to a small group of readers; a guidebook on how to do genealogical research in Virginia would be of use to a broader audience.

Pinpoint the main subject matter of your book (e.g., a nineteenth-century diary, Civil War letters, a guide to cemeteries in your county), and then build upon it.

If you plan to write a family genealogy, think about how far you will include female lines. Deciding to include these lines will mean many more surnames to research. Nevertheless, it may be the right choice if none of the family histories has been previously compiled or if you are dealing with a group of interrelated families.

Be sure to do a "literature search" beforehand to make sure you do not fall into potentially embarrassing traps: (1) you republish outdated or erroneous information because you did not locate the correct updated information [typically about the origin of the family]; or (2) you do extensive original research, only to find after your book is published that another author published the same conclusions decades earlier — and you have reinvented the wheel.

When preparing a genealogical manuscript for publication, you should consider *presentation of research*; *style guidelines*; *organization of the parts of the book*; and *design and printing considerations*.

Presentation of Research

Structure of Your Book
It is worth considering your options as to structure before you start writing your book. Seeing representative samples of various types of genealogical books can give you valuable ideas as to how you want your book to look, and may suggest additional features that will improve it. Indeed, you may want to look at several different samples before deciding which structure suits you best.

Some structures for family genealogies are

- Compiled genealogy of descendants to a certain generation, with personal choice dictating how far to go into female lines;
- Compiled ancestral lines, or a single line of ancestry, perhaps with siblings in each generation;
- Family history with historical context in addition to genealogy;
- Family history based on one or more family sources such as diaries or letters;
- An "all my ancestors" funnel-shaped framework, of yourself or an ancestor, presented in *ahnentafel* format, or as a report with charts in which you would be numbered as 1, your parents as 2 and 3, etc.; or
- Hourglass or double-funnel format, where both ancestry and descent are plotted from a single individual, who would be located at the center of the hourglass.

Other genealogical books may include some elements of the preceding list, such as

- A biography with compiled genealogy. Often the genealogy serves as an appendix to the general biographical work, though this is not always the case.

- A local history with compiled genealogy. For example, numerous New Hampshire local histories come in two volumes: one of town annals, and the other of genealogical histories of town residents; or

- Personal memoirs with a genealogy. This is particularly inviting for those who have been professionally successful and who may wish to ascribe some part of that success to their immediate or extended family.

Enhancing the Presentation

For any genealogical book, you will want to present your material as clearly and as helpfully as possible. Headings or "running heads" in books usually have the name of the book on one page and the short title of the chapter on the facing page; this tells the readers "where they are" in the book.

You can greatly enhance a genealogical book with well-chosen illustrations, photographs, charts, tables, and maps. These will break the monotony of the text and help the reader understand the meaning of the text. They can emphasize the context in which a family lived, often much better than words can. Seeing examples of documents and forms adds greatly to a guidebook. Yet breaking up the text too much can cause the reader to lose interest. For example, abstracts of long documents may be included in the text but the entire document would be better placed in an appendix.

A critical part of enhancing your book's relevance is the title. The title should encapsulate the overall scope of the book. Using a subtitle can augment and elaborate on the title as well. The more accurate you can be in describing the scope of the book, the more readers will be attracted and satisfied with what they find inside.

More Tips for Family Genealogies

From the outset of the project, you should consider your publishing options. You will want to get as much of your work into print as feasible since this is the most efficient and effective way to make your findings known. Your motivation should be to inform family and others about your genealogical discoveries. You will not get rich by writing most types of genealogical books.

In compiled genealogies and other books where specific genealogical data is examined, you have to make editorial decisions about how much narrative to include about specific persons. A rule of thumb is to give more attention and space to those whose accomplishments in life are noteworthy; however, you might wish to devote more space to those who are closest to you and to your own extended family.

You should not be afraid to ask for advice. Generally speaking, people who have been through the research and publishing processes are more than happy to reflect on their experiences. They have gained perspectives that the uninitiated cannot yet anticipate, and they can be valuable guides for navigating around possible difficulties. Their intervention may prevent some typical problems, such as insufficient documentation or adopting an unwieldy project with untenable or unrealistic scope. Don't think because a book is "just for the family" that others won't notice poorly executed research or lack of documentation — or even comment unfavorably in an unsolicited book review.

Another important step you should consider before setting pen to paper is drawing up a big chart outlining the entire family as you are going to examine it. This is useful because it gives you a blueprint for how to proceed, and it gives you visual clues as to how much work remains to be done. The chart helps keep track of individuals, their generation, and their individual numbers.

Finally, it is important to share information with family members. Often this is the only way you can get further information. However, be careful. Research drafts have been shared with family members, only to have them appear later on websites, and often without proper credit. This can be discouraging for the legitimate author, and it can easily provide disinformation if the material is altered or becomes outdated. Communication, as has been said, is irreversible, and spurious information can spread like wildfire on the Internet.

For further reading, see Patricia Law Hatcher, *Producing a Quality Family History* (Salt Lake City: Ancestry, 1996).

Style Guidelines

When writing your book, it is important to develop a plain, effective writing style. Developing your own **style sheet** is also useful. A style sheet is a listing of special terms and constructions you use in your book that should be treated consistently throughout. It may be as simple as listing the preferred spelling of certain words, such as email and website. It may show how you treated an unusual situation that occurs only a few times in the book. Or, it may be a recurring stylistic choice. For example, are you referring to a married couple as Michael and Grace (Halstead) Barstow, or as Michael Barstow and his wife, Grace Halstead? And if you are using the latter style, do you refer to the wife alone as Grace (Halstead) Barstow?

For recommendations and guidelines relating to style, please refer to Chapters 1 and 2 of this book.

Organization of the Parts of the Book

It is important to organize your genealogical research not only carefully and accurately, but also logically. The book's preliminary material, or "front matter" should include the following:

- table of contents
- list of abbreviations
- list of illustrations
- acknowledgments
- foreword or introduction
- preface

The body of the text should be presented in a clear format so the reader can readily understand the contents. Indeed, you may want to include in the front matter a brief section on "How to Use This Book." If you are writing a family genealogy, you will want to study Chapter 2 of this book about *Register* style, which can be used for books as well as articles.

The book's "end matter" should include the following [if the list of abbreviations is long, you may want to put it here]:

- appendixes
- glossary of terms [if needed]
- bibliography
- index

Use appendixes for material that is too long for the text or that is related useful information. For example, a guidebook might have an appendix on relevant contact information including names, addresses, phone numbers, email addresses, and URLs. This makes it more useful and more "user friendly."

If you have used many sources for your book, a bibliography is probably a good idea. Your footnotes will include many short-title citations, and in a book they are apt to be so far removed from the first full citation that it is annoying to have to look for them. In addition, an entry in the bibliography might include your evaluation of the source and suggestions for using it. Generally, all entries in the bibliography should be alphabetized by the author's surname. Some authors prefer to arrange different types of sources in categories in the bibliography.

One absolutely essential part of any genealogy, regardless of length or formality, is a good index. Without a good index, the reader will not be able to access your carefully researched and compiled information. Include every single name in the index. Also consider including place names and subjects, to help the reader.

Design and Printing Considerations

Once a manuscript is accepted, the publisher and author will decide how the book will be designed and printed. Many options are available, due largely to the advent of desktop publishing. Through this technology, both large and small publishers can typeset, design, or scan photographs for any book "in-house," shortening the production process and greatly reducing costs.

The publisher and the author may collaborate to decide upon the design of a book. The design relates to how the text's elements will look when they are typeset. The design includes what fonts are chosen for the text and the headings within the chapters. The design also includes how the chapter opening pages will look, how many photographs will be used to illustrate the book, etc. The type of book will dictate whether it will have a simple or more complex design.

When the book is ready for the printing process, the publisher may again collaborate with the author to decide how it will be bound, the quality and consistency of the text paper, the quantity to be printed, and other related factors. The expense can vary widely depending on the type of paper and binding chosen, as well as the book's budget and its audience. Obviously a paperback book will be less expensive to produce than one that is hardcover and clothbound. A publisher obtains price quotes from printers and then oversees the printing process to ensure that the final step in book production is completed in a timely, accurate, and efficient manner.

NEHGS Book Publications and Newbury Street Press

Most publishers select the works they can produce based on the following factors: (1) the number of books produced in any given year; (2) subject matter; (3) the quality of the work; (4) budget; and (5) estimated sales revenue. It is important to recognize these issues when you are submitting your work for publication.

NEHGS BOOK PUBLICATIONS publishes approximately six to eight books a year, the majority of which are guidebooks for aiding genealogical researchers, like *Shaking Your Family Tree: A Basic Guide to Tracing Your Family's Genealogy* and *A Guide to Massachusetts Cemeteries.* NEHGS  Book Publications also publishes a few books that are more scholarly in nature and are mainly purchased by libraries. An example of this type of book would be *The 17th Century Town Records of Scituate, Massachusetts,* a three-volume set.

NEWBURY STREET PRESS, founded in 1996, is the special publications imprint of NEHGS. Its mission is to produce quality compiled family histories that have enduring importance for genealogists, historians, and researchers. The Press produces approximately twelve books a year, which are often financially endowed by members of NEHGS. In this manner, to serve its authors, Newbury Street Press differs somewhat from a traditional author-publisher relationship. Newbury Street Press consults regularly with highly accomplished scholars in the field of genealogy, as well as devotes much attention to the overall design of the book as a material object suitable for being passed down to future generations of a family.

CHECKLIST FOR "WRITING GENEALOGICAL BOOKS"

- ☑ Think about using your research to create a book with new, useful, and accurate contents.

- ☑ Consider different options for the structure of your book.

- ☑ Look at representative samples of books.

- ☑ Start looking for potential illustrations, constructing appendixes, and seeking other enhancements.

- ☑ Ask for advice from people who have already published genealogical books.

- ☑ Develop a style sheet as you begin to write your book.

- ☑ Organize your book logically to make it "user friendly."

- ☑ Make sure your book is indexed well.

- ☑ Discuss design and printing considerations with a publisher.

APPENDIX

Some Abbreviations and Acronyms Used in Genealogy

This list is intended to help readers interpret the many abbreviations and acronyms used in American genealogy now and in the past. Several of these abbreviations are no longer in use and/or are not recommended. Two journals, NGSQ and PGM, now use practically no abbreviations.

Some abbreviations may appear with an initial capital letter, depending on the context. Some Latin words and abbreviations may or may not be italicized. Some letter abbreviations and acronyms appear with or without periods. A few appear only without a period (e.g., DAR) and a few appear only with periods (e.g., O.S.). For acronyms, it is good practice to write out the name in full at first use, followed by the acronym in brackets.

adm./admin.	administration
admr.	administrator
ae.	aged [*aetatis*]
AG	Accredited Genealogist*
APG	Association of Professional Genealogists
b.	born
bp./bap.	baptized
BCG	Board for Certification of Genealogists[†]
bur.	buried
ca./c.	about [*circa*]
CAILS	Certified American Indian Lineage Specialist[†]

calc.	calculated
CALS	Certified American Lineage Specialist[†]
cem.	cemetery
CG	Certified Genealogist[†]
CG(C)	Certified Genealogist (Canada)[‡]
CGI	Certified Genealogical Instructor[†]
CGL	Certified Genealogical Lecturer[†]
CGRS	Certified Genealogical Records Specialist[†]
ch.	church/children
chr.	christened
CLS	Certified Lineage Specialist[†]
co.	county
col.	column/colony/colonial
coll(s).	collection(s)
comm.	committee
comp.	compiler/compiled
ct.	court
d.	died
DAR	Daughters of the American Revolution
dau.	daughter
decd.	deceased
dist.	district
div.	divorced
d.s.p.	died without issue [*sine prole*]
d.y.	died young
ed.	edited by/editor/edition
ED	Enumeration District/Election District
exec.	executor
f./fo./fol.	folio
FASG	Fellow of the American Society of Genealogists
ff.	and following pages
FGS	Federation of Genealogical Societies
FHL	Family History Library
fl.	alive during [*floruit*, "flourished"]
fn.	footnote

FUGA	Fellow of the Utah Genealogical Association
gen.	genealogical/genealogy/generation
GPC	Genealogical Publishing Company
GRS(C)	Genealogical Record Searcher (Canada)[‡]
g.s.	gravestone
hist.	historical/history
ibid.	same as the preceding citation [*ibidem*, "in the same place"]
IGI	International Genealogical Index
inst.	instant [in the current month]
int.	intention [marriage intention]
inv.	inventory
LC	Library of Congress
LDS	The Church of Jesus Christ of Latter-day Saints
lic.	license
LR	land records/deeds
L-s-d	pounds, shillings, pence
m/mo.	month [in Quaker dates]
m.	married
MD	*Mayflower Descendant*
MQ	*The Mayflower Quarterly*
MS./ms.	manuscript
MSS./mss.	manuscripts
n./nn.	note(s) [as in footnote(s)]
NARA	National Archives and Records Administration
n.d.	no publication date
NEHGR	*The New England Historical and Genealogical Register* [see *Register*]
NEHGS	New England Historic Genealogical Society
NGS	National Genealogical Society
NGSQ	*National Genealogical Society Quarterly*
no.	number
n.p.	no place/no publisher
n.s.	new series
N.S.	New Style [date]

NYGBR	*The New York Genealogical and Biographical Record* [see *Record*]
obit.	obituary
o.s.	old series
O.S.	Old Style [date]
p./pp.	page(s)
passim	at various places in a cited portion of text [*passim*, "here and there"]
PCC	Prerogative Court of Canterbury
PERSI	*Periodical Source Index*
PGM	*The Pennsylvania Genealogical Magazine*
PR	probate record(s)
PRO	Public Record Office
pt.	part
pub(s).	published/publication(s)
r	*recto* [on the front of the page or the right hand page]
rec(s).	record(s)
Record	*The New York Genealogical and Biographical Record* [see NYGBR] or *The New Hampshire Genealogical Record*
Register	*The New England Historical and Genealogical Register* [see NEHGR]
rem.	removed
repr./rpt.	reprint(ed)
res.	resided
rev. ed.	revised edition
Rev War	Revolutionary War
RG	Record Group
ser.	series
sic	thus [indicates a word misspelled or wrongly used in the original]
Soc.	Society
supp.	supplement
supra	above
TAG	*The American Genealogist*
TEG	*The Essex Genealogist*

TG	*The Genealogist*
TR	town records
trans./transl.	translated by/translator
transcr.	transcribed by/transcriber
ts./tss.	typescript(s)
twp.	township
ult.	*ultimo* [in the preceding month]
unk.	unknown
unm.	unmarried
unpub.	unpublished
v	*verso* [on the back of the page or the left-hand page]
v./vs.	versus
var.	variant
vol(s).	volume(s)
VR	vital records
w.d.	will dated
wid.	widow
w.p.	will proved
y-m-d	years, months, days [for age at death]

BIBLIOGRAPHY

- Board for Certification of Genealogists, *The BCG Genealogical Standards Manual* (Orem, Utah: Ancestry Publishing, 2000).

- Bunnin, Brad, and Peter Beren, *The Writer's Legal Companion*, 3rd edition (Reading, Mass.: Perseus Books, 1998).

- *The Chicago Manual of Style*, 14th edition (Chicago: University of Chicago Press, 1993).

- Costello, Margaret F., and Jane Fletcher Fiske, *Guidelines for Genealogical Writing: Style Guide for The New England Historical and Genealogical Register with Suggestions for Genealogical Books* (Boston: NEHGS, 1990).

- Curran, Joan Ferris; Madilyn Coen Crane; and John H. Wray, *Numbering Your Genealogy: Basic Systems, Complex Families, and International Kin,* National Genealogy Society Special Publication No. 64 (Arlington, Va: National Genealogical Society, 1999).

- Fryxell, David, *How to Write Fast (While Writing Well): A Guide to Speed, Organization, Concentration, Problem-Solving, and Creativity* (Cincinnati: Writer's Digest Books, 1992).

- Hatcher, Patricia Law, *Producing a Quality Family History* (Salt Lake City: Ancestry, 1996).

- Kozachek, Thomas, *Guidelines for Authors of Compiled Genealogies* (Boston: Newbury Street Press, 1998).

- Mills, Elizabeth Shown, *Evidence! Citation & Analysis for the Family Historian,* (Baltimore: Genealogical Publishing Company, 1997).

- Mills, Elizabeth Shown, ed *Professional Genealogy: A Manual for Researchers, Writers, Editors, Lecturers, and Librarians* (Baltimore: GPC, 2001).

INDEX